Cycling with the Dragon

Cycling *with the* Dragon

Elaine Woo

NIGHTWOOD EDITIONS
2014

Nightwood Editions
P.O. Box 1779
Gibsons, BC V0N 1V0
Canada
www.nightwoodeditions.com

COVER DESIGN: Carleton Wilson
Images courtesy of vintageprintable.com

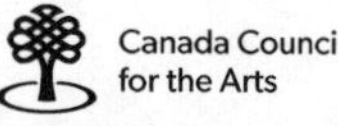

Nightwood Editions acknowledges financial support from the Government of Canada through the Canada Book Fund and the Canada Council for the Arts, and from the Province of British Columbia through the BC Arts Council and the Book Publishing Tax Credit.

This book has been produced on 100% post-consumer recycled, ancient-forest-free paper, processed chlorine-free and printed with vegetable-based dyes.

Printed and bound in Canada.

LIBRARY AND ARCHIVES CANADA CATALOGUING IN PUBLICATION

Woo, Elaine, author
Cycling with the dragon : poems / Elaine Woo.

ISBN 978-0-88971-301-7 (pbk.)

I. Title.

PS8645.O475C93 2014 C811'.6 C2014-905166-2

For my two Daniels and Zen
and in memory of Eileen

Contents

1

2

1

Word Babies

skin aflame   in dire need of dousing

needles lodged in pores   head a thrumming drum

emerging from the canal

out slide you   a swarm of siblings

a throng of reading witnesses   nodding their heads

newborn cells resurface injured building blocks

sinews unclench

The Enemy

under our Grand Teton Mountain
oil reproduction's stare:
dimpled green couch   cognac coffee table
gamboge carpet   static-blighted TV eye
autumnal print curtains

my orange ball   scorches
from little brother's hands
to my hands   hot potato vectors   amputates
Mom's white, ceramic crane-from-tree-trunk vase perch
porcelain bird splinters
into a wintery hail

bombs crater earth

shrapnel shards rain razors

Nanjing—mortar detonates dominance

Mom strains across rice fields

each step threatened by suctioning mud

burrows from Japanese rapacity

stomach acid a violent sea   jostles for gruel

she raises a defiant fist

cracks clay-hard knuckles down

on infringing culprit

daughter's scalp

Sleep: Not Really a Reprieve

from age seven fluorescent green

petulant airborne snakes

dive-hunted me

epoch night after night

sky splitting at the seams neon snake #1 Mom's face foams forth

a shaken carbonated drink

fiery she arcs her head

cutlery tines of forked tongue wounds

You buried any chance

I have of a meaningful career

sliming electric-glow snake #2 is three-headed:

first topped with spiked brown hair, angel skin, goatee

second a squeezed lemon expression, char-black freckles

third mouldy spots, tattooed, multiple piercings

third hisssses, *Who's the most stacked?*

first's tongue drills the air

Hide, go ahead, hide behind

your umbrella

second: You have to repeat

grade one!

I fly inside my skull—my only helmet

enduring double-winged snakes

soaked me in flighty

perspiration

swelled in my core

a changing pupa of desire

to stifle serpent alarm bells

my shut eyelids   Red Sea part

cider light   ear-ringing silence

drenched sheets

Virtue of Smallness

Shattered clamshell fragments

pave the crescent shore

loose mosaic tiles

barnacle cone houses

and soft-skinned

bladderwrack bulbs

pinky-wide to the big toes

of hard-hatted clams

bear scars but are unbroken

by ocean's hammer-fist

Guardian Angel

wrapped in shrouded darkness I seesaw upright in my top bunk

hot curds   hurtle from my depths   incinerate my throat's mucosal lining

dumps a swamp on my blanketed lap

stink puts me on high alert

neon arms of my clock read *3:20*

Dad floats in my   gaping door

wordlessly he gathers up my putrid blanket

fluffs out feather comfort over my small body

his winged spurs cross the sky

They Eat Dogs

The Chinese eat dogs
don't they? my friend asks,
her eyes round
as peppermints.

Heat infuses my face
pomegranate red.
What can I say?
My dad, from Canton,
confirmed that some Chinese
do eat canines
when I was no taller
than a St. Bernard.

I look at my friend's bacon-pink
T-shirt. *Don't you eat pork chops*
every Saturday night? I quiz,
my vision narrowed
licorice strings.
Only plant foods
pass through my lips.

NO DOGS AND CHINESE ALLOWED

Those legendary words
framed the entrance to
a park in British-ruled Hong Kong.

Perhaps that's why
some Chinese eat dogs.

Mom Substitutes

After-school hours: my bed, my Thoughtful Spot,
shifted time and locale from Pooh Bear's

Enid Blyton, my hot chocolate adventure nanny,

Lewis Carroll, a Dali for my imagination,

Louisa May Alcott, Joplin-burn-architect of Jo:

these authors, my familial tribe.

Daily, I nest in the plush of my comforters
and word cloak of my adopted family.

These authors demure: never wielded
a wooden feather duster handle
across my eczema-prone skin, unlike mother.

I'm a conscientious objector—refuse to do my sums
vie for A-pluses, jockey for a turn as teacher's pet
until my literary nutrient-intake
swells my belly, quiets my rashes.

Jo inspired me to backfire
at my vicariously living parent,
Comparisons are odious!

My Dessert

on tissue

I trace filaments of ink drawings from *Harriet the Spy*.

My notebook: A yield

my confidante infinite

my dessert I extract

Reflection: skim

my Harriet

modus tofu

operandi I tote

coconut tofu a concealed journal

I Wonder If I Too...

Spiders weave streamers of grey webbing

the length of my ceiling beam

hoping to capture sustenance

I wonder if I should grow six

extra legs

spin silk nets

Heron at Lonsdale Quay

Great heron, on the dock
surveying pools of oil shine.
Backdrop: red and black burnished tugs.
All is calm, all is bright.
Your lustrous eyes scan deception
below your feet.

Will you keep vigilance over
the upright two-legged
rather than the finned?

蓝斯代尔码头的苍鹭

硕大的苍鹭哟，你是在哀悼
清洁大海的失去麼？
淡然伫立在码头上
水边是一片一片的油渍。
远处有红黑相间的拖船
闪闪烁烁。
不可能有健康的鱼类。
你专注的目光扫视着
脚下的污浊。
但愿你在上面巡视
用你的双足，而非你的翅。
或许你威严的身形会
唤醒他们的敬重之心
正如你唤醒了我的一样。

(Translation by Changming Yuan)

Seal at Maplewood Mud Flats

Brown mermaid,
your slick body ripples,
weaves through waves
dashing on the pebbled beach.

Then, only the retracting tide.
Will you weather humankind's violations?

枫木泥滩边的海豹

棕色的美人鱼呵，
你光滑的躯体波动着
穿游在冲向卵石海岸
的波浪中。

然后，只有退却的潮汐。
你会在人类的侵扰中
继续生存麼？

(Translation by Changming Yuan)

Unresolved

In French 8,
he slips his hand
in my desk and sneaks off
with my journal
incroyable my secrets

He taunts:
"I know about the birthmark
on your thigh
your 30-double-A bra
you have the hots for
you-know-who
the gaunches your grandma
irons at the laundromat
How big are your
mother's feet?
Does your dad still
wear a braid?"

I envision bursting out of
the phone booth of my shyness
cape flaring in the wind
and flying fearlessly to
vanquish this villain
but day after day he erodes me
delicate as stressed old bones
I fragment
Elavil knits me together again

Sometimes though, old
fractures still splinter
then sky, trees, fence whisper,
"How big are your feet?

Bet you wear a braid"
The air sprouts lips,
screams, "Ha ha ha"

Difference United

laying before me   waterfall froth   dark ripples

a white sailboat   and navy blue fishing boat

marina   bundle of toothpick masts

cottages   concrete box houses huddled

on elbow of shore

tiger's eyes of lights

on the pier

blinking into the settling dusk on the hem

of the deciduous-skirted mountain   steady drizzle cleat-clicking on

my porch

a display of the distinct and differing

heritage of nature and humankind

by the rocky shore   an exhale of awe

mist rising to meet appeased clouds

the sky dappled in smoky hues

a motorboat's wake follows

its owner's path to the pier

Bustling Gold

before the birth that is spring
I was in the woods a couple of times
with someone whose chatter shoved
my mind from sensing
today alone an open stage in the narrows
the tide low revealing expanses of sand toes
water hill loaves give rise to space inwardly
I can let the breeze bewilder my hair
walk at a lazy pace drag my runners
I see a clam clutched in a sky-laddering seagull's beak
warningless its catch plunges
its despair a spoiled baby whimpering
ducks motor westwards
I clutch this momentary catharsis
from the constraints
of suburban inbreeding and density
shaving cream foam from the river mouth
reminder: shave my legs some day or not
suited sailor birds tootle
at waterway's throat

more sky-farers   flying confetti

saplings stretch arms

reaching for spouses across the trail

forming an awning for the sojourner

I return   accompanied only by a train's complaining

I see lime fur lining the path

the static in my head dimmed   I return to the jazz

at the entrance   don't stop at the feeders

two joggers in fluorescent gear enter as I leave   rare birds

Garment Tags

If I wear yellow

shall I conjure up garb

of isolation and exclusion?

Stitch coats of distressed fabric

I've sustained from white lacerations?

Shall I wear shoes heeled in tradition?

Shall I don dresses of ancestral expectation?

Pull on diaspora pants?

Or if I wear white, shall I surmise

my classical Greek toga is everybody's textbook?

Or strut my skin as fashion's only line?

Or patch myself from different lines

into an approximation of truth?

Tree

Outstretched arms   green digits
radiating into the violated atmosphere
rickrack for the Bargains
Galore concrete torso
I, beetle, lift
my face to the ozone
hole bared sun
shoppers trickle
from the super-sized box
loaded with parcels of *Shop Now,*
No Interest for 6 Months deals
unmindful of concrete miniscule
soil triangles anchoring
my loft in this asphalt football field
except while reverse-angling
their fossil fuel elephants
mega-tires butt-printing mud

Feathers Powdering the Air

I glimpse her by the grain terminals
from my car window
she, a Canada goose, lies
inverted on the pavement,
body tilted, black head,
slender neck crooked,
white belly, so Styrofoam-like,
feathers powdering the air,
black feet webs dangling.
She, the one who couldn't
get away from the reversing
boxcar chain by the grim
frigid waterfront.
Her kith and kin, ignorant
of the guillotine potential
of metallic wheels, roost
still on the tracks as iron grates
on relentlessly.
Their wings: possibility.

2

The Hood

grey hooded skies
I'm on the phone
encircled by evergreen spikes
my neighbour says
writing is just your hobby
not your real work
my eyes walk up
to the chalk dusting of snow
blanching Mt. Seymour's apex
she continues   I *never*
have pots and pans piling
up in *my* sink
she   as myopic as the neighbour

who said   homemakers are kept women

boiling sour waters at my feet
I'm reading the brown park lawn
cloud turmoil
creek water spitting
wet darts pierce

Service Sunny Side Up at the Recycling Plant

I mainline curried lentils on roti
leapfrog into my Toyota Tercel
tread on the gas
sandwich my car between the bosses' Bimmers
step in the entry, pucker my eyes
at boot marks on the floor and walls
tail a sun shaft to the yard and pit
where forklifts are bears

Leapfrog into my Toyota Tercel
collide with the voices of my supervisors
step in the entry, pucker my eyes
at boot marks on the floor and walls
tail a sun shaft to the yard and pit
where forklifts are bears

Collide with the voices of my supervisors
At the top step, into the white-lit room
bearing the world, I slump up the stairs
my phone is calling already

At the top step and into the white-lit room
I buttress myself for the words,
"My recycling wasn't picked up."
I adopt my sugar voice
I buttress myself for the words,
"My recycling wasn't picked up."

Sandwich my car between the bosses' Bimmers
I adopt my sugar voice
I main-line curried lentils on roti

He

I, hunter-gatherer—am I Dagwood
to your Blondie?
How about a kiss and hug
this morn' before I speed
off to toil and forage?

Your work is stress-free and serene.
Childcare? House care?
Easy, peasy... no dog eat dog

On return from the wilderness
I need hot chow, flicks, order...

What have you been doing all day?

Tumblers in Blondie's mind click,
lock in place: picket signs loom
in her brainscape

Lady See:

Orcas spy-hop,
poke heads above the water,
leap and land back-side atop waves
lob-tail and pec slap,
roll on their sides
to smack a fin
on the sea's surface,
trill, whistle,
grunt, snort air through
blowholes, squeak,
moan and creak a dialect.

Lady Do:

I slide down in my tub
Only head and neck protrude
above water's surface.
I lounge amidst bubble floes,
crash foam islands
filter after steam-comfort
up my nostrils,
cook abstractions
in cerebral contemplation.

With Word

Ascent to Quarry Rock and composing poetry are pregnancies:

anticipation,

eruction slopes and chasms in physical and psychic terrain,

crossings over log bridge mood gullies,

panting up vertical.

Mt. Seymour lies like the convex of my belly,

ocean beneath my skin,

at mountain's knees.

With child, with word, with umbilical cord

to creation.

We Perch on the Edge

Hand sanitizer antisepticizes
visitors' hands preceding entry
to the glass room
I cross the threshold, my gown blue,
and face anxiety-coloured
day after day.
My eyes are wells,
lips, compressed traitors.

For you, I'd walk the length
of the Baden-Powell.
Babe, you are but the length of my hand,
swaddled in a heated cube;
your electronically brained ward.
Electrodes at your stub shoulders
clamp on umbilical cord stump.
Red and shivering,
vernix still clings to your brows,
mats your sideburns and hair.
Your half-moon forehead
guards a brain
not yet patterned to resilience.

Clenched eyelids lock out the world.
Birth weight: that of a litre of milk.
Your mouth and eyes are
hyphens and question marks
in your yet-to-be-told tale,
nose, your blue pencil
as I stroke you
with the accordion vinyl gloves
stretching into your vitrine hurdle.
I wonder what your eyes see
when I feather-brush your forehead.
I gurgle to you,
make like a fish
mouth you kisses
you can't feel.

Outside, the rain is driving nails.
You and I,
we perch on the edge.

Peace on Earth: Cacophony

How are you?

I'm a mess.

Don't come near me. Don't see the girls. Only you can make this Christmas not ugly.

He parked in our carport and didn't say anything. We didn't know whose car it was so I called a tow truck. Then he called a few days later and said....

There was an oil tank in our yard. We had to have it removed. The soil's all contaminated. It'll be very expensive to remove.

The kitchen's so dirty, you're going to attract bugs. You'll see. Cockroaches. Ants.

Out of the Box

My dream, the late, late show, projects onto my inner mind's screen.

My man is
clad in a white
shirt and tie.
We are at YVR.

Take-off to a landscape
with an army
marching through
tall office blocks

The army morphs: both women and men clad in civilian clothes
march amidst office towers. The women cavort in Pucci-print
mini-dresses, white go-go boots; the men, button-down shirts,
grey flannel.

I'm in liquid trousers, white man's shirt, hair an unwound flannel bolt.

Kitchenitis

My relationship with my kitchen is a psychic malady.
Dishwasher door yawns open.
I empty the cutlery rack, formal forks
in official drawer, old reject forks
in for-cooking-use drawer.
I've just deposited spoons in their shower stalls.
Two pots weep steamy torrents.
Drawers hang open awaiting their occupants.
I rotate the scrub brush round bowl base.
I can't fathom the build-up of pots, bowls,
Rubbermaid containers and plates in the dishwater soup.
I garburate chicken back bones
as carrots and potatoes bubble angry.
I slide beef cubes in grinder's receptive mouth,
dump Styrofoam packaging. Reprieve in sight?
Alas, no. Rinse children's plastic cups,
undress cans of labels, aluminum ribs bare, bath-ready.
Stew pot has steam issuing from its head.
Portabella—ready to dive in? I'll scrub your caps first.
Shaving you is more tiresome than spinning gold into straw.
Your flat deck casing into the blue box.
I can't help but release a black sigh.
When will this end?
Maybe the day I roll into Sunrise Assisted Living,
my meals arrive on wheels.

Descent

wind-chimes   crystals clap   a song

for you   I regret I've been   remiss

a period   long as the Nile   since I've visited

I won't let such mileage   separate us   again

I'll clean your grave marker

sweep all   the errant leaves   away

clip the grass that   impinges on   your state

I'll make   this a   ritual

I try   to beat the sinking sun   I forgot

to bring floral offerings

Mom

the dusk is   descending

Ma

I married her son

She tells me my necklace
from the Sally Ann
is the ugliest thing she's ever seen
the beads would be more useful as buttons
No point in my going to school—
won't result in a paying job
My house smells of dust,
my kitchen is malodorous;
she pinches her nostrils shut

She says, her voice scraping the ceiling,
arms windmilling, how crazy I am

        A year after our son was born she paid
        for the help who swept our rugs
        and coddled baby

She tells my son I'm a bad mother, fingers
his long hair and slight arms,
rotates him like a roast,
asks if he's getting A's in school

When my mother embraced her angels
I gave her shoes to Ma
A week later, the shoes tagged $6.99 in
the bargain bin amidst faded shirts
and pants in Ma's grocery store

Chinese New Year, I buy three pricey
vacuum-sealed duck breasts for her
gift-wrap Walker's shortbread
keep a red bag to deliver them in
yet refuse to celebrate with her
Mid-March, I enjoyed the buttery wonders alone

I greet her name on the call display by
walking away

I think she's a window and I can see her innards

When we took her to Paris she was quiet
lost in the landscape
language, currency, maps, Metro
          Not so transparent
She rallied to her old self, ventured
the cherubs painted on a palace ceiling were skin-ugly-naked

She gives me a present—
a marble mortar and pestle
but she's the one who loves to cook
her recipes have endless permutations

She shadows my mind's eye
          Ma striding up her hotel's stairs
          pink sweatsuit enveloping her like rose petals
          white hair, a bird's nest, swept over her bald spot
          broom in one hand, toilet bowl brush in the other

Soulmate

rain does all the talking today

its wet slides along my skin

softly glides down my ears my neck

slips inside my hiking boots

kisses my feet

a tug lit as though by bioluminescence

laboriously pulls a rusty barge;

a mouse hauling a dinosaur across moiré

gulls loiter round pylons

geese ply

the milky sky

lack of birdsong

an empty sleeve

my soulmate

the rain

Night-time Symphony

The riled wind jangles
my sterling chimes
metal rods jive
clang percussion
argue
collision
    external

I cosset myself in my house
in my room
hear the dryer's tumbling
my timpani accompaniment
    internal

    Then, a lullaby

    flute notes of the night train's whistle
    churning turbulence of a jet

    tom tom of raindrops on my skylight
        without

    pad, pad, padding of the clock's second-keeping
        within

    ease of my mattress

The Naturopath's Receptionist

She salivated over the diamond
and gold ring sets the good doctor's clients wore.
It was three years counting since they wed.
He had typhooned past the jewellery store.
Never mind, she didn't care about bling bling.
The fashion mags in the grocery store racks said,
Keep your love life alive by hugging
and kissing your lover day after day.
She shyly told him this with a gift of his fave:
a jar of pickled onions and they did,
but after a week and a bit
they were too sandwiched for time every day.

Three weeks before Valentine's she hinted
a bouquet would be oh so nice.
Two weeks before she said, *Even a single*
rose would suffice.
The day of, she pleaded, *Show me you love me.*
They took the bus to the grocer's.
She relented, *Wait till we're rich.*

From Christmas until Easter he initiated
intimate relations once,
or was it actually twice?
She fretted he preferred men but no,
not the case.
He found gay love repellent,
maybe another day.
She loved pleasure
so asked him if she could use
mechanical aids.
No, he said his lips clamping closed.
He did not have religious restrictions
but suppressed his libido
just as he constricted his consumption of meat.
She hoped in time,
she too could learn the same as he.

Glow the Night

rain dit-dit ditting

finger and thumb snapping

a thousand rain tears of joy

on window face

leaf and cedar footprints

beacon streetlights

glow the night

mind's moonbeam

on silence   stillness

freedom from shackles

fulfilling unbridled pleasure

of imagination roaming

If Shoes Made the World Turn

In Freemont

a brunette shimmies
out of
a boutique gyrating
like Tina Turner
feet enfolded in ankle booties
Aren't I sexy?! she crows aglow,
undulating in her white mini.

If it were only so easy to make
all the perishing Carl Solomons
of this planet
feel sunny-sky-high.
Alas, they would be shod, but still un-whole,
not beyond the brittle of ego.

Mirror Mirror

Is it all about being a mirror?
I say, *You have little hands* He says, *You have a little face*

Image I cast Image I cast
Leaving grimy dishes in the sink
a leaning tower
papers skewed asunder
on my desk as though bothered
by a storm
peaks
of books on the
dust-coated coffee table
ferreting out stray keys
ten minutes late
not on the key ring
not under the lambkin sweaters
where, oh where?

Yet this seedling of mine
of his own volition
scrubs the cupboard doors
asks if I've been nice
to the Rottweiler neighbour
repeats, *Sorry, sorry* to friends
for a minute's tardiness

I am you You am I
I am I You am you

3

In the Making

For years I shaped art
by weaving, twisting and threading
cherry, wine, blue and amber
into earrings, bracelets and necklaces.
As I beaded through dark and light,
an inner whisper,
anxiety on a gnat's insistent wing
flew into my consciousness:
was this seemingly innocent,
pleasurable crafting
using minerals chiselled
from Hadean depths,
a ripple that added to the waves
devastating the forests,
lakes and rivers?

I knelt through one morning's murk
with my bowl of rainbow stones,
stringing turquoise and white.
There was dirt on my upturned palms.
It dawned on me that my craft was sullied,
my pretty rocks might be no better than
blood diamonds.

An image of words came,
strung on the wire of syntax,
hung loosely around my neck.

A Nod to Myself

done dicing oyster mushrooms

slicing pork and turkey meat into slivers

scrambling soft egg whites for fried rice

serving young one and spouse

hearing out my teen's hour-long recounting

of a fantasy game

my legs rubber bands as I ascend the stairs

gently shut the bedroom door

lay down and draw a blanket of silence

and darkness over my torso

horizontal for minutes   I feel myself ebbing back

my true being a potent amalgam seeping up my circulatory system

from feet to scalp   genuine as my red cowl-neck sweater

and faded jeans

I slip into my 6' × 10' private room

to fountain pen document in black and white

my experiences   my processes   give a nod to myself

the stretch waistband of freedom-giving

Blue

Your salted wounds

as if you to breaking strain

a piano with its hammered keys

and rusty bolt revolt

an ode to you

who must whisper-stroke the ivory

coax music from pain's dark holt

Crying

She erupts in drought peaks and flood phlegm, ozone skin lesions from Arctic head to Antarctic toes, innards slashed for silver, diamonds and gold to prettify her human inhabitants. People orally rape her with plastic islands, exhaust and chemical runoff. Her oil is milked of every drop till her nipples crack and dry. Her seas are dynamite-fished and leached with radiation and mercury, her forests clear-cut. Mama's organs are her health gauge.

This poem is flesh, blood and sinew.
Flesh, blood and sinew will be legs for Mama.

End of Pretty

my friend Rachel only thirty-something
hunts for raiment
that doesn't make her
seem more sprout tender

she says my fifty-plus hands
look young I ask her what that means
not crepe-y betrayed
not sun-ravaged
not arthritic bloated
my indelicate fingers
thickened with dough kneading dish rinsing
seem to reverberate
are no more glass-fragile
but more limb-bark anatomy
than the smooth octave-spanning hands
I had before cross-hatching crisscrossed my brow
leopard spots bloomed on my cheekbones

Lost & Found

I max out my Visa reach for debit

I eat avocado oil chips and dark chocolate

I rest on my egg-crate foamy

I struggle to chat with an narcissist friend

I rub my turbulent lava belly

I unearth solace erudition in my page-traversing pencil

Word Mirror

She says through safe telephone distance,
Why is it that Chinese Persian and Indians
are always in the news for committing crimes?

My words my brass shield deflect her inflammatory spears,
Are Willy Picton Clifford Olson Ted Bundy and Charles Manson

Chinese Persian or Indian? I ask.

I know she's winding her verbal arm back

ready to chuck more weaponry.

She replies, *They're all mentally addled.*

I mouth-mirror her lopsidedness and say,
How do you account for the Hell's Angels
the Mob or the Bacon Brothers?

She flounders in silence her psychic image and delirium refracting

back in soundless piercing shards from my looking-glass retort.

R
A C

DAY ONE
SCENE ONE
[Camera: *Establishing shot*]
[*Action*]
an alabaster forearm
propels a carton of fries
from truck window
[Camera: *Cut to*]
[Sound: *Actual sound*]
smacking on turbaned head
blood ketchup dribbling fury
[Action: *Beat*]
potato curls cling
to white cloth
[Camera: *Break the bubble*]
black diesel fart embeds
[Camera: *Cutaway*]
[Camera: *Follow shot*]
I of citron skin witness
driving behind the truck
utter a vow to alter this tale's closure
[*It's a wrap*]

Heart Bypass

In a pharmaceutical company whirlpool
drugs are available
to erase guilt, tinker with conscience.
So far, only administered for
post-traumatic stress
but if obtained and made dispensable
as lattes or smoothies,
I fear legions of sociopaths
who could kill without a horse hair of regret,
maim women or children or those minus
similar noses, eyes, gender or god.

Would fear and logic still
bodycheck the remorseless?

Cordova & Dunlevy

Her mouth a black
hole reminiscent
of the one
in Edvard Munsch's
The Scream.
She twists
from side to side,
witnessing a horror
manifest.
Cars roar past,
their drivers
with eyes fixed
straight, mouths
horizontal
lines.

Season Off-key

I walk through yellowed grass
heads in repose
sapling arches
brackish uprooted
bamboo stalks
sullen stands
youthful morose trees wave
asthmatically
wheeze
catching swell
and fall
of breath
the sea laments
an off-key murder of crows
traverses a dust-grey sky
helicopter a raucous bird
beats its blades
hovers

I dream of you, hospitalized
my brouhaha heart beat
I happen upon
red and green canes
Santa ornaments
a black string-around-the-finger reminder
of called-for cheer

bulrushes curtsy
low
a black and white chickadee needle

weaves deftly
in and out

of blackberry textile
across the inlet belly steam belches

from the Shell refinery

Feminine Ecology

For the beauty of strong, creative women is "ugly" by misogynistic standards of "beauty." The look of female identified women is "evil" to those who fear us. As for "old," ageism is a feature of phallic society.

– Mary Daly, *Gyn/Ecology: The Metaethics of Radical Feminism*

My body's ecosystem: mammillae
dormant, non-lactating,
filaments of lichen over
the mysterious cavern,
tunnel of life, former pleasure,
voluptuous belly,
residue from joy
of doubling,
legs, fluid,
arms, twining vines,
head, a peak that weathers
fires, storms and calm alike,

all kindling for discovery

and self-reclamation

birthing the linguistic

explore the contours

of the universal.

My Brother

Like a litany I tell him,

Put a third coat on the fence panels
with two coats. Put a second coat
on the inside panels. Call me when
you're done.

He needs to lie down first.

He's had to rouse his paralyzed
parent, spoon-feed this man, aid
and abet him in dressing, ablutions,
and toileting.

After that, fax an eviction
form for his janitor mom.

Others in the family deem
him "unemployable."

They complain he takes twice as
long, is stubborn when he
shouldn't be, doesn't listen and
has no memory.

He drags his left foot like
a tail. Injury, an accidental
consequence of medication.

But when he applies luxurious
strokes, those wooden boards drink
in his sincerity, a compliment
to his artistry and deem him
"good" as I do. Appreciating him
more than the God he zealously
worships.

He gyrates more than a
jumping Mexican bean
thump thump thump
shoving the deck bench back
against the house with a
wham wham wham.
Spasms, an inheritance
from prescribed drugs.

He's waiting for me to drive him
home to

Pain & Hastings.

Ride Along East Hastings from the Patricia Hotel to Woodward's

I ease up on pedalling, periscope my head high
above the ram's horns handlebars.

I see you, on your knees
in front of the Carnegie Library
puppy dog panting eager for crack nirvana
to erase your fissure deep pain.

I see your potato nose,
pock-cratered skin, chaotic hair
wheeling your Safeway cart world—
sleeping bag, sweaters, jackets
and third-time-round Adidas
aching for a safe place to stop and name "home."

I see you in spaghetti straps
and strawberry silk
at the corner
as needle skinny
as the ones that track your arm.
Temptress's stance, knee bent, leg poised on tiptoe
starving for the solace-food that never comes.

I see so many,
slouched in line at the other Sisters'
where turkey rye, steaming veggie soup and God are served.

I arrive home.
I roll into the rungs
of the giant red-enamelled
steel dish rack assembly
and loop steel cable security
through the wheels.
I try to will the elevator
to rocket me fast
to my sixteenth-floor suite,
turn the double-pronged tongue
of my door.

The Chinese say everybody
in the world is their brother or sister,
but this trip
earthquake of my fastidious universe
open gash of humanity.
I swan dive under my two-hundred-thread count
snowdrift-white comforter
and like a snake swallowing eggs
down orange pills that keep my voices silent—
the only distance that keeps me from being one of you.

Source

sun in quilt patches

on our Japanese acacia,

blocks of light and shadow on red

revs circulation   shimmer my cheeks

glisten my clavicle

Acknowledgments

Deepest thanks to my family for putting up with me for squirrelling away for many a winter and summer while I completed this manuscript.

A heartfelt thank you to Anna Jean Mallinson, Carol Shillibeer, Cole Swensen, Eugene Kaellis, Isaac Yuen, John Asfour, Madeleine Thien, Ray Hsu, Silas White and others I may be remiss in mentioning for reading through specific poems or drafts and for editorial advice.

Thank you to Carleton Wilson for the fabulous cover design of this book.

Special thanks, too, to the editors and publishers of the poems that have appeared in other literary spaces.

A version of "Virtue of Smallness" appears in *carte blanche*, Issue 20, 2014.

"They Eat Dogs" and "Unresolved" were workshopped respectively at Christianne's Lyceum in Vancouver and by Montreal poet John Asfour during his residency at Historic Joy Kogawa House before publication in *Ricepaper Magazine*, Fall 2010. Both pieces have been performed at the Word on the Street Festival in 2010 and 2011 and subsequently in other venues in Vancouver.

Versions of "Ride Along East Hastings from the Patricia Hotel to Woodward's" have lived many lives. It was set to music in collaboration with composer Adam Hill at the Art Song Lab, Vancouver International Song Institute, in 2011, premiering as the keynote piece at VISI's "Playing with Fire Concert" the same year. As an art song, it has been performed at St. Andrews-Wesley Church and the Canadian Music Centre, both in Vancouver in 2012. It was first published in *Ascent Aspirations Magazine* in 2009 and then republished in *V6A: Writing from Vancouver's Downtown Eastside* in 2012.

Versions of "With Word" and "Feminine Ecology" were published in *Ricepaper Magazine*, Fall / Winter 2012.

"Ma" came to life in *V6A,* Arsenal Pulp Press, 2012.

English language versions of "Heron at Lonsdale Quay" and "Seal at Maplewood Mud Flats" were published in *The Enpipe Line* in 2012. Both pieces were read during a protest reading with contributors Fred Wah, Stephen Collis, Renée Saklikar, Kevin Spenst, Mercedes Eng, Reg Johanson and Marilyn Belak at *The Enpipe Line* launch outside Enbridge's office in frigid March weather in 2012. I had both poems translated into Chinese by poet Changming Yuan to reach across cultures.

"Night-time Symphony" began as a poem and was set to music by composer Daniel Marshall at the Art Song Lab, VISI 2012. Good fortune has shone on the art song version by way of a festival award from the Boston Metro Opera, 2013.

A version of "Difference United" is online at worldpoetry.ca.

"Word Babies" is online at Bone Orchard Poetry.

About the Author

Elaine Woo is a poet/librettist and non-fiction writer. Her work has appeared in *ARC Poetry Magazine, Shy: An Anthology* (2014 silver medal winner of an Independent Book Publishers (IPPY) award), *V6A: Writing from Vancouver's Downtown Eastside* (a finalist for the City of Vancouver Book Award in 2012), *The Enpipe Line, Earthwalk, Ricepaper, West Coast Line, Ascent Aspirations* and *Megaphone Magazine*. Elaine's art song collaboration with Daniel Marshall, "Night-time Symphony," won a Boston Metro Opera festival prize in 2013. Born in Saskatchewan, Elaine is now a resident of North Vancouver.